My dreams are all I own, I counted them to nobody but you, you are my refuge when I am unhappy, and even if I am "frank" and crazy my best pleasure is to be your best friend

Storm make trees take deeper roots, and going through them with you makes my life a wonderland...

♥ Research has shown that laughing with your best friend for 2 minutes is just as healthy as watching you do it LOL ♥

If more of us value what is precious
cheer and friendship would be
above hoarded gold...

Just because you are angry it doesn't mean you stop your inner power of being silly, and I am concidering that the best things in life are silly...

You are a magical person, your
beauty is beyond compare, if I am
always around you is because you
worry for me and you always care,
therefore I love you and I don't
mind, because good friendships last
for a lifetime.

I made a little experiment, I always try to cheer myself singing and found out that the only thing better than singing is singing with you!

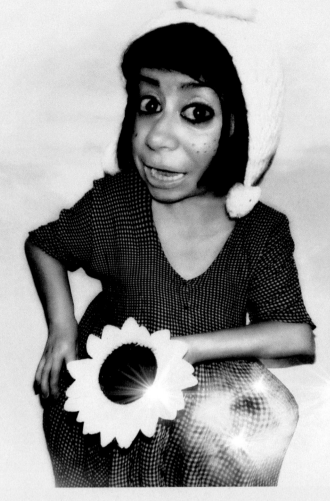

This world is full of
magic, and my magical
place is to be next to
you...

Blessings comes in various ways, the most
beautiful comes in the form of a person like
you...

Friendship is the most important magic ingredient in life's recipe ...

Any friend who isn't happy
when they see a clown is an
enemy infiltrated in the
circus ...

I'm happy because you can see the good inside of everything...

Never loose your sparkle because
you make me shine...

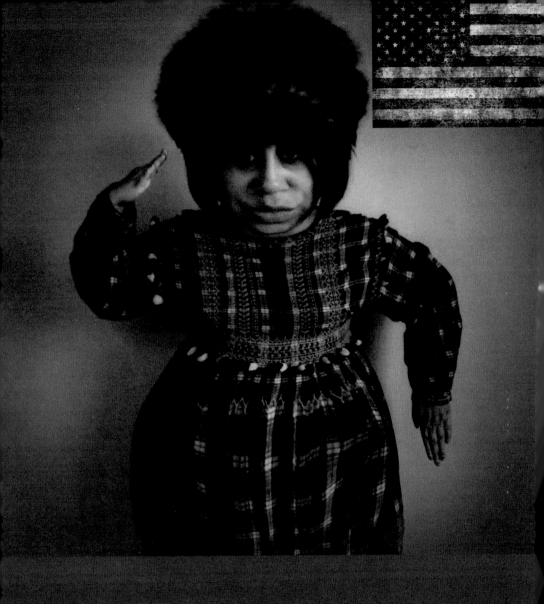

I stand before the flag
because my American beauty
just arrived...

A smile is round it has no end, that is the reason you are my best friend...

Friendships look out for you and you never know, that is the reason you see a UFO...

True friendship is not about being inseparable but about being able to be separated without anything changing ...

Remember a bad grade doesn't define your future, good people always learn something new and I learn a lot of things with you...

Life is short, smile at those who cry, ignore those who criticize you and be happy with who you care about

The genie always says one thing that applies to you, your wish is my command ♪

If I had one wish in the world.
I would choose your
friendship...
that is enough words to say

When words fail the music
speaks and you are my
music

*No matter what they tell you, remember you are the princess of this tower... that means nobody can defeat you*

Put your hand in mine we are
from heart to heart sweeter than
candy and that last forever and
ever...

Even if you are a magic bully, your
kindness would be your
superpower...

Blow your sorrows and
embrace your
happiness...

There is always a brightside
when I am next to a troll...
you!

I hope you like my message and I hope you care
because our friendship is better than a love affair...

You are the reason
someone smiles
today...

Made in the USA
Columbia, SC
06 February 2023

11607789R00018